PAUSE ||

A Diversity, Equity, and Inclusion Journal

Introduction Written By Angela Chiarenza

Illustrations by Wade Forbes

PAUSE ||

A Diversity, Equity, and Inclusion Journal

Introduction Written By Angela Chiarenza

Illustrations by Wade Forbes

Print: 978-1-7368912-5-4

Layout and Design by Trembling Giant Marketing, LLC.
www.TremblingGiantMarketing.com

Angela dedicates this project to Amelia. Amelia's ever-steady presence creates an inclusive environment of love, safety, creativity, and joy.

Wade would like to dedicate his artwork to those who are taking these conversations further than the day before. May these illustrated quotes and blank pages create space to pause and ultimately shift conversations into new directions. This project is also dedicated to his supportive family. All our walks in the woods (to pause and think) made these quotes come to life sooner.

Introduction

"This moment is more precious than you think."

I saw this quote when I was a kid, written with chalk on a sidewalk in New York. I have never forgotten it, and it always comes to mind at just the right time. This quote tells me that I always have the ability to choose, to decide to make the most of a moment.

Decision points occur throughout the day, giving us an opportunity to react or decide. I can react to something, and often find that after it occurs, I wish I had responded differently. I have also discovered that if I take a deep breath before I respond, I have the opportunity to decide how I move next, what I say, and the tone and quality of my response.

When I was 10, a friend screamed a homophobic slur in my face. It scared me, it was hurtful, and I did not know what to do. I recoiled and froze in fear. Since then, homophobic slurs have been yelled in my direction while driving, while sitting at dinner amongst friends, and while walking my dog. I have lost count of the number of times I have been standing in line to use a public restroom and been told that "the men's restroom is over there." In each of these situations, I have felt unbalanced.

Sometimes I am scared, other times I am angry, and every time it is hurtful. Though these experiences are unpleasant to say the least, they also give me the opportunity to pause, take a deep breath, and decide how to respond. I am grateful for the times in my life when I have had the wherewithal to pause, take a deep breath, and appreciate the moment.

I met the love of my life in a boathouse; I have had the good fortune to build friendships with teammates, workmates, strangers, and neighbors; and I have been present for the births of babies and the passing of loved ones. Each of these moments is precious to me.

Including this moment.

When I was in my early thirties, I met a colleague stuck behind a desk, with an inspiring artistic talent, who had a sense that he was not making the most of his moments. Nearly a decade later, that colleague, Wade, published his first of several illustrated journals. And now, he has asked for my input on this journal, tapping into my experiences to augment the creative illustrations you see in these pages. In the days since our time working together, Wade and I have had hours of conversations about life, relationships, work, kids, dogs and cats, tractors, good markers, the best paper, hard stuff....joy. The list continues.

We are humbled to bring you this journal.

We invite you to join our conversations in the safe space of this journal. Our hope is that you bring your whole self to its pages. Take a deep breath. Pause. And, let it all out with ink onto the pages.

Let us know how it goes; what you think. We can't wait to meet you.

How This Journal is Meant to be Used:

Did you know that journaling will:

Lighten your load and give you a place for heavy thoughts?

Allow you time to study yourself, habits, goals, thoughts, and emotions?

Reduce stress, expand your vocabulary, improve your emotional intelligence, and boost memory and comprehension?

Throw your ideas and questions onto the pages to deepen your reflection. Around each illustration is a space for you to doodle, dream, and draw. Imagine that, at the end, you won't be the same person you were when you started. Show kindness to yourself and see what happens. Notice mistakes in the drawings in this journal, which were left on purpose, because no one is perfect. Take a moment to reflect on what you learned and what you'll take with you into your next conversation.

"HATE
IT HAS
CAUSED A LOT
OF PROBLEMS
IN THIS WORLD,
BUT IT HASN'T
SOLVED ONE YET."
—Maya Angelou

Parking lot

① Timeline + process
- look @ end to end and understand
- evaluate
- Expectations + timeline needs
- JULY (Bree + Rocio)

v-team

Experimentation

Feature planning

July 31 Looking forward

Lotus

Lakshmi   Kelly + Rael

Nancy   Pedro

Procurement

Blake

Dex

Testing

5

"AN ELEPHANT WHICH KILLS A RAT IS NOT A HERO."
—African Proverb

"IF YOU ARE FORTUNATE TO HAVE OPPORTUNITY, IT IS YOUR DUTY TO MAKE SURE OTHERS HAVE OPPORTUNITIES AS WELL."
– VICE PRESIDENT KAMALA HARRIS

WF.22

GAME PASS

Campaign Management — Recio + Boyd

S   D

D   CD   BAT   VP

— BB	— KW
— AP	— AG
— BM	— ME
◯	— GB

DELIVERY
+
OPTIMIZATION

I want to continue learning. when

Lead on plan post mortem

Plans arent being shered

Long range planning

WE DO NOT REMEMBER DAYS. WE REMEMBER *moments.*
-Cesare Pavese

18

"AND STILL, AFTER ALL THIS TIME, THE SUN HAS NEVER SAID TO THE EARTH, "YOU OWE ME". LOOK WHAT HAPPENS WITH LOVE LIKE THAT. IT LIGHTS UP THE SKY."

-Rumi

TOMORROW IS PREGNANT AND NO ONE KNOWS WHAT SHE WILL GIVE BIRTH TO.

–African Proverb

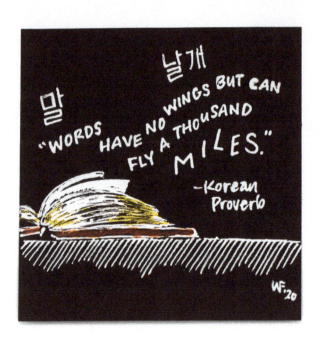

WISDOM COMES WITH THE ABILITY TO BE STILL. JUST LOOK & JUST LISTEN. NO MORE IS NEEDED. BEING STILL, LOOKING, & LISTENING ACTIVATES THE NON-CONCEPTUAL INTELLIGENCE WITHIN YOU. LET STILLNESS DIRECT YOUR WORDS & ACTIONS. - Eckhart Tolle

WF '21

"THERE ARE NO BIRDS IN LAST YEARS NEST."

~Henry Wadsworth Longfellow

FOR TOMORROW BELONGS TO THE PEOPLE WHO PREPARE FOR IT TODAY.

—African Proverb

"THE ONLY PERSON YOU ARE DESTINED TO BECOME IS THE PERSON YOU DECIDE TO BE."

—Ralph Waldo Emerson

"THOSE WHO ARE THE HAPPIEST ARE THOSE WHO DO THE MOST FOR OTHERS."
—Booker T. Washington

NEVER STAY UP LATE FOR SOMETHING THAT WOULDN'T BE WORTH GETTING UP EARLY FOR.
-Unknown

"THE SOLE MEANING OF LIFE IS TO SERVE HUMANITY." -Leo Tolstoy

BORN INTO SLAVERY, BIDDY MASON SAVED ENOUGH
MONEY TO BECOME ONE OF THE FIRST BLACK
LANDOWNERS IN LOS ANGELES. SHE EVENTUALLY
MADE NEARLY $7 MILLION IN TODAY'S MONEY—
AND GAVE IT AWAY TO CHARITY.

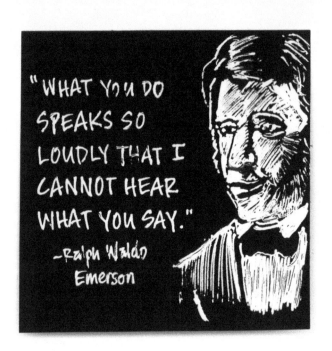

"WHAT YOU DO SPEAKS SO LOUDLY THAT I CANNOT HEAR WHAT YOU SAY."
–Ralph Waldo Emerson

"AFTER ALL IS SAID AND DONE, A LOT MORE WILL HAVE BEEN SAID THAN DONE."
—unknown

"IF THE FIRST WOMAN GOD EVER MADE WAS STRONG ENOUGH TO TURN THE WORLD UPSIDE DOWN ALL ALONE, THESE WOMEN TOGETHER OUGHT TO BE ABLE TO TURN IT BACK, AND GET IT **RIGHT** SIDE UP **AGAIN**."

-Sojourner Truth
May 29, 1851

W.21

"FINISH EVERYDAY AND BE DONE WITH IT. YOU HAVE DONE WHAT YOU COULD – SOME BLUNDERS AND ABSURDITIES NO DOUBT CREPT IN. FORGET THEM AS FAST AS YOU CAN [FOR] TOMORROW IS A NEW DAY."
— Ralph Waldo Emerson

I LOOKED AT MY HANDS TO SEE IF I WAS THE SAME PERSON.

-Harriet Tubman

IT IS EASIER TO
BUILD STRONG
CHILDREN THAN
TO REPAIR
BROKEN MEN.
-Frederick Douglass

IF YOU
WANT
TO FLY,
GIVE
EVERYTHING UP
THAT WEIGHS
YOU DOWN.
—Unknown

WF-21

"THE COLOUR OF SKIN IS IN NO WAY CONNECTED WITH STRENGTH OF THE MIND OR INTELLECTUAL POWERS."

—Benjamin Banneker

SOMETIMES YOU NEED TO TALK TO A TWO YEAR OLD JUST SO YOU CAN UNDERSTAND LIFE AGAIN. —Unknown

"HISTORY HAS SHOWN US THAT COURAGE IS CONTAGIOUS, AND HOPE CAN TAKE ON A LIFE OF ITS OWN."
– Michelle Obama

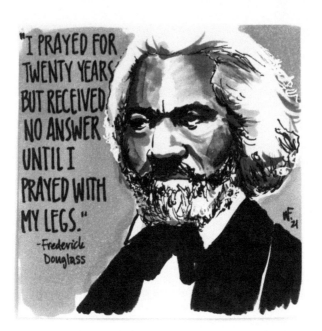

"I PRAYED FOR TWENTY YEARS BUT RECEIVED NO ANSWER UNTIL I PRAYED WITH MY LEGS."
—Frederick Douglass

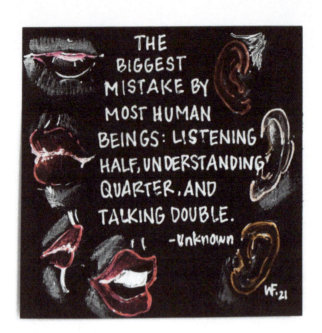

THE BIGGEST MISTAKE BY MOST HUMAN BEINGS: LISTENING HALF, UNDERSTANDING QUARTER, AND TALKING DOUBLE.

-Unknown

WF.21

"OCCASIONS WHEN YOU CAN CHANGE YOUR MIND SHOULD BE CHERISHED, BECAUSE THEY MEAN YOU'RE SMARTER THAN YOU WERE BEFORE."

— Malcolm Gladwel

THREE THINGS CAN NOT BE LONG HIDDEN: the sun, the moon, and the truth.

—Unknown

"LISTENING IS AN ART THAT REQUIRES ATTENTION OVER TALENT, SPIRIT OVER EGO, OTHERS OVER SELF."
~Dean Jackson

"LAUNDRY IS THE ONLY THING THAT SHOULD BE SEPARATED BY COLOR."

—Author unknown

WF '21

"IF I HAD ONLY ONE HOUR TO SAVE THE WORLD, I WOULD SPEND FIFTY-FIVE MINUTES DEFINING THE PROBLEM AND ONLY FIVE MINUTES FINDING THE SOLUTION."

—Albert Einstein

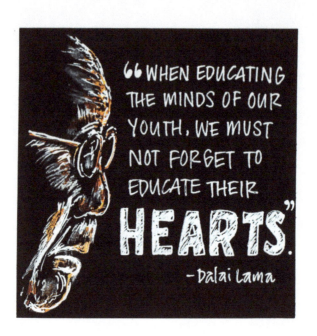

"WHEN EDUCATING THE MINDS OF OUR YOUTH, WE MUST NOT FORGET TO EDUCATE THEIR HEARTS."

—Dalai Lama

"YOU CAN HAVE IT ALL. YOU JUST CAN'T HAVE IT ALL AT ONCE." - Oprah Winfrey

"ALL THE DIVERSITY, ALL THE CHARM, AND ALL THE BEAUTY OF LIFE ARE MADE UP OF LIGHT AND SHADE."
—Leo Tolstoy

"FEAR IS A REACTION. COURAGE IS A DECISION."
~Winston Churchill

WF 12

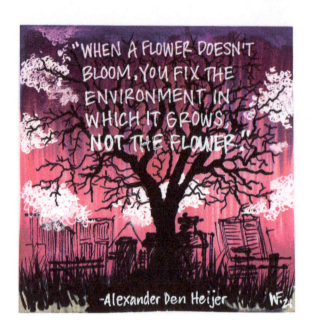

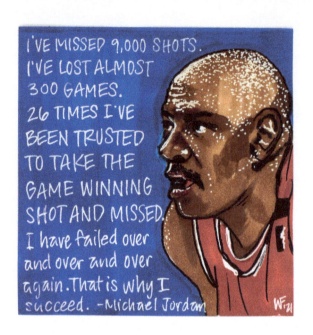

I'VE MISSED 9,000 SHOTS. I'VE LOST ALMOST 300 GAMES. 26 TIMES I'VE BEEN TRUSTED TO TAKE THE GAME WINNING SHOT AND MISSED. I have failed over and over and over again. That is why I succeed. –Michael Jordan

"WE BECOME NOT A MELTING POT BUT A BEAUTIFUL MOSAIC. DIFFERENT PEOPLE. DIFFERENT BELIEFS. DIFFERENT YEARNINGS. DIFFERENT HOPES. DIFFERENT DREAMS."

—Jimmy Carter

WF. '21

"THERE IS ONLY 1 WAY TO LOOK AT THINGS UNTIL SOMEONE SHOWS US HOW TO LOOK AT THEM WITH DIFFERENT EYES." —Pablo Picasso

WF·21

"READ ABSOLUTELY EVERYTHING YOU CAN GET YOUR HANDS ON BECAUSE YOU'LL NEVER KNOW WHERE YOU'LL GET AN IDEA FROM."
—Malcolm X

WF.21

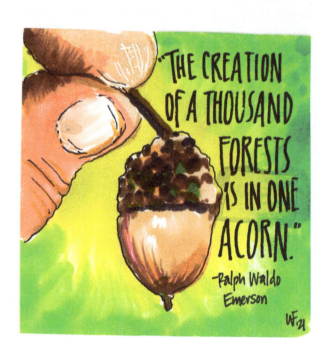

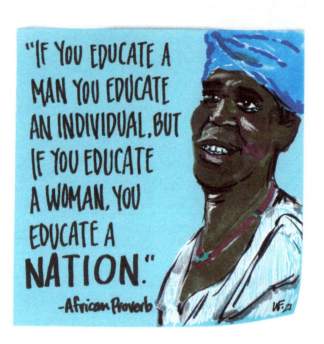

"IF YOU EDUCATE A MAN YOU EDUCATE AN INDIVIDUAL, BUT IF YOU EDUCATE A WOMAN, YOU EDUCATE A NATION."
-African Proverb

Art is the most intense mode of individualism that the world has known.
—Oscar Wilde

W.21

I am two of the most POWERFUL words, for what you put after them shapes your reality.

"TAKE ALL THE RULES AWAY. HOW CAN WE LIVE IF WE DO NOT CHANGE."

—BEYONCÉ

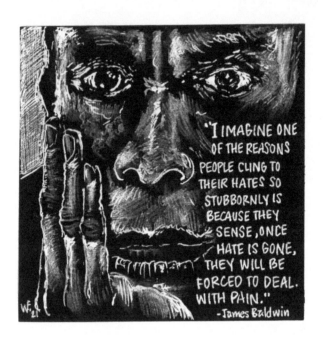

"I IMAGINE ONE OF THE REASONS PEOPLE CLING TO THEIR HATES SO STUBBORNLY IS BECAUSE THEY SENSE, ONCE HATE IS GONE, THEY WILL BE FORCED TO DEAL WITH PAIN."
-James Baldwin

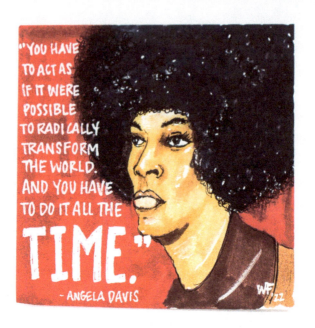

"YOU HAVE TO ACT AS IF IT WERE POSSIBLE TO RADICALLY TRANSFORM THE WORLD. AND YOU HAVE TO DO IT ALL THE TIME."

– ANGELA DAVIS

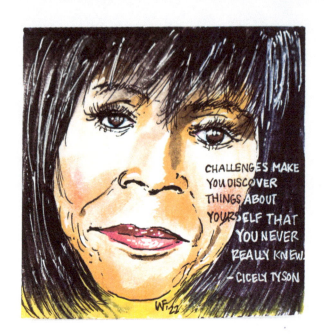

CHALLENGES MAKE
YOU DISCOVER
THINGS ABOUT
YOURSELF THAT
YOU NEVER
REALLY KNEW.
— CICELY TYSON

—Barack Obama
20 January 2009

Acknowledgements

Projects like this are not accidental and require being open to new things.

Wade would like to thank the strong people in his life who have offered him the courage to draw these quotes. Ellsworth "Brownie" Brown, you helped him understand more about the world and our lives in every conversation. Rommel "Rome" Wilson, for our conversations about race, tribes, and our upbringings that unearthed new perspectives. To his wife Megan, for helping him find the right words and giving him seven tries to say something in a better way. To his sons, for helping him wrestle with concepts and recognize the value of bringing this journal into the world. To the countless people in his network, who have commented on his illustrated quotes throughout the COVID-19 pandemic and offered enthusiasm and grace for these important topics. Lastly, to Angela, for agreeing to embark on this project with him when he mentioned that he had "a bunch of quotes that I think would help improve conversations."

Angela would like to acknowledge the dedicated, passionate, teachers whose energy and perspectives have inspired this journal. Those teachers have come in the form of teammates, educators, coaches, friends, students, peers, colleagues, and bosses. Gratitude runs deep.

Notes: